I can still smile
like Errol Flynn

I can still smile like Errol Flynn

Tito Titus

Empty Bowl Press

Copyright © 2015 by Tito Titus

Cover and book design: Nina Noble Design
Cover photo: Damian Lee, taken at Gallery Faire Café, Seattle
Set in Berkeley Old Style, designed by Tony Stan

ISBN 978-0-912887-36

Library of Congress Control Number: 2015949668

Printed in the United States of America

EMPTY BOWL PRESS a division of
PLEASURE BOAT STUDIO: A LITERARY PRESS
201 West 89 St., 6F
New York, NY 10024
Tel / Fax: 888-810-5308
www.pleasureboatstudio.com / pleasboat@nyc.rr.com

for Kate

There is a life and there is a death,
and there is beauty
and melancholy between.

Albert Camus, *Notebooks*, 1935-1942

Contents

Is this a good time?

Someone's darling daughter   15
McKenzie River   16
33 years   17
Club Crow revisited   18
The little imp   19
Nose hairs   20
Wide pants   21
White lace bikini   22
The noise in the hallway   23
Found mind   24
Beauty and pain   25
The beginning of great sadness   26
Morning has broken   27
Just down the hall   28
When I am on the internet   29
Anne Carson and me   31
Benny the lawn mower   32
The house on Cornwall Street   33
Haunting Bolinas   34
Flies   36
Dear Meghan   37
Annie visits Mr. Phillips   38

Nicole visits George   39
Green doors   40
Can you hear me now?   41
The evening of the day after things changed   42
Hells Canyon homecoming   43
The aspen affair   45
This island earth   46
Winter harvest   47
The First Noble Truth   48
The Gahan Wilson Comedy Hour   49
Monday morning coming down   50
B.B. King, Eric Clapton and me   51
Mr. Pokey   52
Generations   53
Paradise lost   54

The beasts within

Things that go bump in the day   59
My father's nose   60
Broken   61
My parents' house   62
Historias acera de mi padre   63
Baptizing Dad   66
It seemed like a good idea   67
Last flower   68
She up and died   69
St. Joan   70

Swish of a horse's tail

Cigarettes and wine   73
Davey's dance with the devil   74
Eddie Cotton, interrupted   75
The pianist   76
With both feet on the floor,   77
The murderer upstairs   78
Tucson   79
A terrible mistake   81
When first they met   82
The end of summer   83
Wisdom of the wind   84
When Buddha Dog died,   85
Dog gone   86
Lamplight lamentation   88
What a lovely way   89
These times   90
Another one   91
Remembering Frank   92
Remembering George   93
Better late than never   94
Say goodbye now   95

Notes   97
About the author   99

Is this a good time?

You're older than you've ever been and now you're even older.
And now you're even older. And now you're even older.
You're older than you've ever been
and now you're even older still.

John Flansburgh/John Linnel (They Might Be Giants)
Long Tall Weekend, "Older"

Aging is like enlightenment at gunpoint.

Anna Halprin

Someone's darling daughter

approached me today
with a bag of weed
at a good price,
even for Hilo,
and I said *yes*
because the plumeria
tattoo peeking above
her low slung sarong
told me pleasure
lasts only a while.

McKenzie River

There were moments we glistened
like rushing water on mossy rocks
in Oregon mountain sunshine,
naked, not caring for shade,
laughing, not wanting more.

33 years

> *With these hands, I will bring to you*
> *a tender love as warm as May.*
> Benny Davis, "With These Hands"

On your chest, these hands,
your heart beating our history.

On your feet, your ankles,
San Francisco, Amsterdam, London.

On your mons, our home mound,
forests, river beaches in the sun.

And your belly, white, tender as love,
lentil soup, kombucha, kefir homemade.

On your body, your precious body,
keep these hands, hold on.

Club Crow revisited

I drunk-dialed you
sitting at this bar, this very bar,
plastic laminate faux wood pattern
dissolved from elbow years.

I sat on this same black stool
thinking of you and Tullamore Dew,
not to mention Canadian Club,
when you answered in delight
like this was a wonderful thing.
You knew your voice made
better elixir to shine my day.

I need a fancy-handled knife
to carve your name on Formica,
to mark my Club Crow spot
and remember when was when.

The little imp

He opened the door without knocking.
"What are you doing?" he asked.
I'm trying to remember when I was as young as you.
"Why?" he asked.
Before I could answer, he closed the door.

Nose hairs

He ain't gonna buy one
of them nose-hair scissors,
or one of them little round
things they sell in catalogues
for old folks that got
nothin' better to do than
lookit catalogues.
You know. Them little metal
things shaped like funnels
for filling fruit jars—only
small enough to stuff
up a man's hairy nose
and buzz bristles away.
Naw, that's not for him.
He's gonna do
what he always does:
reach in there with
forefinger and thumb,
grab some hairs tightly
and yank.

Wide pants

I don't know
about these wide brown pants
with the big pockets,
all loose and comfy—

something a man would wear
to feel slack and easy,
like the men who wore coveralls
without having coverall jobs,

or jumpsuits, velour jumpsuits,
maybe green or maroon,
with a zipper up the front,
good freedom for the man.

Oh, Jesus, please, I can't stand it.
Let's settle on vast chocolate
cargo pants with eight pockets,
only sixteen bucks at Target.

White lace bikini

I didn't take her picture
when she stood ankle deep
in the green river water,
her white lace bikini
still dry and loose
on her sepia body.

I didn't take her picture
when she waded deeper,
river water wetting
white lace in sunlight,
flashing pheromones
across shimmering ripples.

I didn't take her picture
but wrote this poem,
stuffed it in my pants.

The noise in the hallway

It's troubling how much noise
three children, two parents,
two grandparents can make
in an apartment building hall
outside your thin wood door.
It annoyed you, I am sure,
like you said when your head
emerged from your entry,
frowning and mouthing
the word *quiet* in the firmest way
a nervous woman can muster.
    You were surprised, I think,
    how we outnumbered you.

I was surprised, too, the day
I passed your door, heard you
coming, glorious heaving releases,
your voice erupting from deep
inside your body, again and again,
only moments before your man
began the same symphony
in baritone bellows, the air
on my side of your door
vibrating in harmony and rhyme.
    I don't mind your noise.
    I rather enjoy it.

Found mind

He lost his Mind
then found it again
years later buried
in an unlit closet
lying on the floor—
beneath Army fatigues
an old blue pinstripe suit
empty Jim Beam bottles
strip-club tickets
and speeding tickets
a woman's red panties
empty cigarette cartons
empty jars of missing things
abandoned foibles and facts
best left forgotten.
His fresh-found Mind,
a little weary and worn,
smiled and said,
What took you so long?

Beauty and pain

She ran with lean
muscles and grace,
a barefoot princess
before arthritis took her down.
Think back—
remember her running
home from the neighbor's?
Wearing short shorts,
long legs leaping
magically over shrubs
in crisp December cold
beneath a full moon,
swiftly up the steps
three steps at a time,
then closing her door
until she couldn't run
like that anymore.

The beginning of great sadness

Winds kick up
blow through my bones
like Torricelli's trumpet.
Dust devils churn my brain.

Diablo dirt whirls,
stymies the light,
makes lonely moans
like the sinking of a train.

Morning has broken

When morning broke it shattered,
not of its own volition.
The evening before, I set it up,
stacking pieces precariously,
balancing neurons on memories,
ganglia tenuously holding on,
soaked in dank fissures of brain.

When morning broke it shattered,
acute shards of regret piercing
my consciousness, hacking at hope
like a vicious Samurai slicing
away my best yens,
like a Sumo sitting on gray
matter that can't breathe.

When morning broke,
so did I.

Just down the hall

Sometimes I am the man
who lives in the apartment
at the end of the hall.
Dim faux crystal lights
spread a weak yellow hue
over thin red carpet
stretched over old wood
not polished in years.

On a Saturday or Friday night,
teetering men or bleary women
knock on my pale door
(holding stemmed glasses
or blue aluminium cans).
They invite me to the party.

I smile, and politely say,
no thank you and thank you
for so kindly thinking of me
at the end of the hall.

I return to my chair,
smudged window and music,
and watch the sun set.

When I am on the internet

> *When you're on the internet,*
> *no one knows you're a dog.*
> Peter Steiner cartoon, The New Yorker

I live in Laguna Beach, California,
own a glamorous downtown gallery
featuring major-name openings
where women whisper my name.

When younger, Columbian
drug lord styling framed
my handsome visage.
Now, my pony tail severed,
I sport sea-salt speckled curls,
and remain drop-dead gorgeous
in an older, South Coast way.

In the cresting Pacific evening
I walk cheerfully straight and tall
along the soft-breeze beach,
smile, nod, and maybe wink
toward lovers in the sand
rolling in sunset colors.

They know my name
from my last gallery show
and with a modest laugh
I autograph her shoulder blade
in Sharpie marker pen, for
she too is drop dead gorgeous
in a younger, Laguna Beach way.

Anne Carson and me

> *Carson did admit ... that part of her desire to learn Greek came from her childhood desire to be Oscar Wilde— classically educated, elegantly dressed, publicly witty. I asked her when she stopped wanting this. "I didn't," she said. "Who could stop? It's unachieved, as yet."*
>
> Sam Anderson, *The Inscrutable Brilliance of Anne Carson*, New York Times

The article you read to me

    the one about Anne Carson—
    that brilliant woman who writes
    through side angles of mind,
    flipping brains with surprises,
    throwing mental curve balls,

made you wish you were smarter,
you said as you laughed it away,
and I, feeling sad, wished
I were younger, making
different choices, following
different paths, becoming
Anne Carson.

Benny the lawn mower

The lawn got mowed today.
The woman went out to mow,
said she loved to do it.
And if you ask me,
I think she does.
It gave me plenty
opportunity to feel guilty,
even though my leg bone's
broken worse than religion,
and what do you know
Benny shows up! Ball cap and
tee shirt, full beard and charm.
He knows us, he says,
because he saw us drinking
at the Black Crow Club.
He wants to mow our lawn
and we say "sure" because
we're good neighbors too,
even though we only have
twenty dollars to pay him,
and he'll need more than that
at the Black Crow tonight.

The house on Cornwall Street

I suppose this isn't a good time
to knock on your door—
twenty years after I never
said goodbye and promised
I would "always be there."
Found your address on an envelope
buried by papers ready to waste,
stuffed it in my pocket
for a couple years more—
as if *you'd* always be there.
Ink bleeds with sweat and time,
soaks the paper in blue ponds
until words blur, the way my memory
dims your voice into mystery.

Maybe one day I will write the letter,
the one that apologizes
for leaving you without a wave
or kiss or word or tip of my hat,
like I could be trusted to return.

Haunting Bolinas

I visit Richard Brautigan's house
in Bolinas, California, on the windy
wet coast north of San Francisco.

I stay in the house at night
where Richard exploded his brains
with a twelve-gauge shotgun.

A woman comes by each night,
stands in the dimly lit walkway
outside the glass entry door,

looks at me in the front hall
her sad eyes asking me a question
I do not understand and I am

afraid to answer the door
because I know I do not belong
in Richard Brautigan's house.

She opens the door with a key,
lets herself in, stands in the amber
entry, tells me her name, Ianthe.

You do not belong in this house,
she says, because you do not
own a Remington pump action.

You don't drink anymore and you
would never do to your daughters
what my father did to me.

Flies

It's come to this, watching
flies at the front window
on a summer afternoon.
Two flies, one on glass,
the other on the ledge,
walk in lazy circles,
perhaps a mating dance,
until a larger fly arrives
strutting the white sill paint
like he owns the window.
The smallest fly remembers
something urgent, leaves in haste
to somewhere free from large flies.
The pane reflects my face.

Dear Meghan

You call me cute. That's sweet.
This old man, grizzled a bit,
sagging slightly at the shoulders—
the gravity of years.
I can still smile like Errol Flynn
and wink but not quite.
So when you call me cute,
I pretend I still have it,
that I still have the stuff
I used to think I had.
When I told you these things,
bent forward, head tilted
in my self-deprecating way,
you decided on *charming*,
more like Cary Grant,
or a man who has no penis,
who women adore
like you say you adore me.

Annie visits Mr. Phillips

*Ya know that old trees just grow stronger,
and old rivers grow wilder ev'ry day.
Old people just grow lonesome
waiting for someone to say, "Hello in there."*
    John Prine, Introducing John Prine,
    "Hello in There"

She came by today
feeling fragile, perhaps only tired,
and he welcomed her,
though feeling fragile, too.

They walked the block,
with the black hairy dog,
made creamy sweet coffee
and hugged goodbye.

She made sure
his door was locked,
his keys were found,
left him alone.

Nicole visits George

He smelled of anesthesia
lying in his hospital bed
feeling faded and forceless
beneath crumpled gray covers,
when you, young beautiful woman,
touched his brown-spotted forearm,
smiled your sunny smile,
touched his eyes with your own
and made him, for a moment,
young again.

Green doors

Green door, what's that secret you're keeping?
Marvin Moore, "The Green Door"

Long ago green doors opened
to parties that happened,
or didn't happen, depending
on a gentle man's memory.

Green doors in old houses
opened to women he loved;
or maybe he didn't know them,
doesn't remember their faces.

The brilliant doors still stand ajar,
bright apple green, chipped paint
confessing coats of other colors—
red, white, and ochre—
lifetimes long past.

Power parties still breathe
fire into young men and women,
sometimes sweet, sometimes dark,
but always hot as loaded loins,

or faded and hazy like a man's
memory of what happened
or maybe happened long ago
behind green doors.

Can you hear me now?

Sunlight through dusty panes
yawns across the kitchen floor,
silently, like the room,
silently, like the house.
A gentle breeze outside
brushes the eaves.

He walks to the fridge,
removes a waxed
box of tropical juice,
listens to the muffled
sound of foaming orange
falling into the glass
like thick chilled sunlight.

The weak wooden chair
creaks as he sits—
a sound in the room
that says you live here
in this empty house.

The evening of the day after things changed like they'd never changed before

He wanted to sit on the front porch
watching no one pass on the empty street,
but it was cold, wet and windy,
so he sat in the darkened room
watching the telephone. It rang once
earlier in the day. A wrong number.
He thought to engage the caller
in conversation but let it pass. Perhaps
someone else would call. Or maybe not.
Or probably not. Or not at all.
The radio played songs he didn't know
by performers he didn't know.
The newspaper still lay by the front door.
He cleaned the refrigerator. It contained so little.
He forgot to turn on the furnace,
put his hands in his pockets and shivered.
At last he reached for the bookshelf.
Sometimes he felt a little bit Leonard Cohen,
but he felt like Bukowski tonight.

Hells Canyon homecoming

These hills
    they're green now,
    but when the dry season comes
    they'll be brown—
    burned toast on a grasshopper's belly,
    fried grass searing in the sun.

These hills
    they got rocks bigger than houses,
    God's public art, black and copper,
    shapes you can't make.
    They mark my memories
    in ways I don't understand,
    ways that make me who I am.

These hills
    they can bring a man down
    in heat of day. People die hiking
    rocky slopes, steep as a tractor grille—
    some, freckled with green pine towers,
    pretend to offer shade to the footsore;
    others, naked as a blistered hog's back,
    do not abide fools.

These hills, amaranthine hills,
    they play the shadows,
    throw them about at dawn,
    across random clefts and crags,
    every morning for millions of mornings,
    before then and after now.

These hills
    they have no memory.

The aspen affair

If a tree could say
"Hey there, big boy,"
it would be the aspen.
She would say it while
shimmying in the wind
beneath a wide western sky.
Her gently rounded leaves
would wiggle and wave
for a man with an eye,
a heart, and a love of the land.
Her tender branches would
bend, embrace the breeze
and reach for the rush
that comes in evening warm.

Pines are spiritual
the way they moan and wail
in the mountain night.
Cottonwoods jabber like crows,
murders of vulgar green crows.
But the sensual aspen,
gently seductive aspen,
knows me too well—
she asks me to stay
and I put my money down.

This island earth

The best place to seek God is in a garden.
You can dig for him there.
    George Bernard Shaw, The Adventures of the Black
    Girl in Her Search for God

Dark rich soil runs
through hominid fingers,
black nutrients wink
at the virgin April sun.
Thick man-fingers grab
handfuls of the stuff,
earth that settles damp
in the palm that packs
the dirt, tamps it in a can.
God in a can.

Winter harvest

It's snowing again
like it did this morning
and the night before.
She cuts a branch
of chokeberries, red
as December ribbons,
hangs them in the window
where the sun shines through.

The First Noble Truth

The doorman at the department store
greets shoppers at the door,
hopeful, craving approval,
beaten down but coming back.
A real job.
Did he know this is where he would go?

A woman, broom in hand,
sweeps sidewalk waste to a pan,
defeated, beaten senseless
by life and dirty streets.
Woman alone.
Did she know this is where she would go?

They were children once,
teens with dreams,
and now so old, lugging wisdom,
submission in their eyes.
What happened? Did she dream
of sweeping streets?
Did she dream at all?
Did they know
this is where
they would go?

The Gahan Wilson Comedy Hour

The television
sits in the room, the empty room,
the darkened empty room.

The television
in the empty darkened room
flicks tentacles of light
across walls of gloom,
illuminates tattered drapes,
peeks through gaping shreds.

The television
watches the empty darkened room,
blinks and winks and smiles.

The television
ate them all.

Monday morning coming down

You can't do wrong and get by.
Lethal A. Ellis, "You Can't Do Wrong and Get By"

Racy red Triumph
burning aflame
freeway off-ramp
sobbing blonde.

"Help me! Help me! I need a ride.
I need to be in court in ten minutes!"

Your car is on fire.
You need to stay.

"No! No! They'll put me in jail, pull
my bond. I'll lose my baby!"

Racy red dress
chassis made to kill
and already dying
before turning thirty.

B.B. King, Eric Clapton and me

I'll be your Eric Clapton if you'll be my B.B. King.

Wanna big ass Cadillac
that'll fulfill my fantasy,
sittin' in soft black leather
stripped from cattle grown
without barbed-wire fencing,
supersound on the radio,
daring decibels blasting,
air-conditioning as quiet
as a vacant cemetery.
The neighbors see and say,
*Jesus Christ, there he goes
in his big ass Cadillac.
Sunnuvabitch, who the hell
he think he is, struttin' stuff
like a goddam rock star,*
and I smile like Howdy Doody,
like I didn't know any better.

Mr. Pokey

Mr. Pokey wants in. Wearing a worn winter coat
in July, he stares through the shop window.
He admires the merchandise—
lingerie, bath notions, sensual gifts
for women. He adores the lovely
sales clerks—the way they laugh, tilt their heads,
sometimes drop their hands slightly at the wrist,
revealing their softness, gentleness, vulnerability.
But their vivaciousness fascinates him most.
If he used the word vibrant, he would say:
"I love their vibrancy."
He doesn't enter the shop. He never does.
On sunny afternoons, he carries weather-beaten
bags down Fifth Avenue, stops at the shop display
only a minute. They call him Mr. Pokey because,
as he leaves their window, he walks so slowly.
He has no idea what they are laughing about.

Generations

On hot rocky summer trails
I wore deerskin sandals and walked naked
on sunburned ridges, through dusky gorges.

My hair grew long,
my beard thick as a bear's pelt,
before it became thin and white.

My body grew lean from steep climbing
and from the hunger that haunted me
when these wild lands did not bless my hunt.

You do not know, you have no way
to know, how I threw the spear,
how I brought down the beasts.

You laugh when I stay near the fire
even in summer, and walk with a stick,
too slow to chase the deer.

Sadness claws at me—knowing you
and your children will have children
who will not know I ran these lofty lands,

a sure-footed goat on sharp rocks,
seed of champions in a new world,
father who killed fresh meat for his family.

Paradise lost

> *Take a little walk with me and tell me: Who do you love?*
> Bo Diddley, *Bo Diddley*, "Who Do You Love?"

Chaise-lounge Chester, red belly
bursting over baggy Gucci trunks,
scowls at the sea beyond the lawn,
like he's grimaced at everyone
since making his first million dollars.
The stone carver called Time
chiseled angry crevices from the corners
of his unhappy lips, glaring eyes,
and across his sunburned brow.

He's swung some deals
that would make *you* frown, too;
pulled cash from a classy hat
that night in Soho, kept C-notes
under his Cadillac floor mat
(passenger side), fixed favors
for no-mailing-address friends;
paid his dues, if you catch my drift.

Did I tell you about Mauricio?
He built a sausage empire,
expanded into fifteen flavors,
beef jerky, turkey jerky, smoked,
teriyaki, home-style, seasoned pork, spicy,
all natural jalapeño bacon,
fifty shades of pepperoni.

Frail at 80, Mauricio decided
to learn to dance—move
his body, arms, and heart like a kid,
flirt with girls on the floor,
smile past next Sunday.
Wet-eyed, he told me,
This is the best thing I've ever done.
I've never been happier.

Chester, listen to me.
The sun is setting, and the worst—
it's over. You're not too late
to take a walk on the beach—
warm ocean water wrapping
your feet to the ankles, trade-winds
brushing your body, clean sand
titillating your toes 'til Tuesday.

Give it a shot.

The beasts within

*They call them nuclear families because
too often they go nuclear.*

Sayings of Te Toh

There was proximity, but no relating.

Elaine May, *Improvisations to Music*, "Tango"

Things that go bump in the day

I was ten. We lived on a farm. We grew onions,
corn, potatoes, and more sugar beets
than stars in our cloudless Oregon nights.
My father drove a pale green '50 Ford pick-up
truck. My mother was cooking my
soon-to-be-born brother in her belly
when my father bumped her with the truck.
Knocked her down.
Seeing her skinned knees and elbows, he laughed,
said it was an accident. She disagreed.
Until the day she died forty-two years later,
she railed: *He did it on purpose*!

My brother turned out fine—
and with a sense of humor better than mine.

My father's nose

Keep your nose clean,
my father would say,
and I thought he meant
stay out of trouble
and maybe he did.
My nose? My nose is clean.
I pick it at stoplights
when there's nothing to pick,
scrub it daily, keep it shiny,
not at all like my father's
dirty nose—with every pore
spotted black by neglect.

As he lay on his last bed
awaiting the great corridor,
gasping for air, gurgling each breath,
I wanted to tell him:
they have nose inspections
every day on the other side.

Broken

A broken whiskey bottle
off Highway 99,
a hollow three-bedroom rambler,
the suburban kind.
Down the darkened hallway,
blood stains, broken vinyl tile
beneath the sagging bed.
She rests her head, ashen.
Her husband's pistol, a .22,
drops from her hand.
Bullet.
Gut.
Monday morning, 10 a.m.

My parents' house

Someone remodeled the house
in my dream last night,
the one I visit so often, the one where
blood ran through cracks in vinyl tile.
They painted the walls white to cover
years of smoke stains and odors,
installed a new white furnace
that looked like a clothes dryer,
and ran quietly like a Cadillac clock,
replaced the tile with shiny hardwood,
left the place clean, sterile,
empty.

Historias acera de mi padre

My father spent his last decade in a Mexican lakeside
village. He lived in a nine-room *hacienda* with lawns
and gardens, pools, fountain, chandeliers, second wife,
gardener, and maid. Hidden behind high bougainvillea-
adorned adobe walls and medieval locks.

Speaking of my mother, he said, "She's not poor. She
has a television."
"I bought that television," I replied. "And my brother
pays her cable fee."
"You see?" he said, "She's not poor."

❦

It began innocently enough. My daughter, wife, father,
and I were having lunch on a sunny hotel patio
in Ajijic, Mexico, near the Lake Chapala shore.
A seductively cheerful guitarist came to sing
at our table. A happy baritone. I enjoyed paying him for
the delight he brought. Excellent food lay before us.
I mentioned—regretfully, if you ask—that I thought
it was interesting how the United States and Mexico
treated separation of church and state differently.
In the U.S., rules address what the government
cannot do, whereas in Mexico the rules dictate
what the church cannot do. He tensed. With narrowed

eyes he asked what I had against prayer in the schools. This surprised me because I hadn't offered any opinion on the subject and because I had always known him to be disdainfully atheist—to keep his intellectual-superiority-badge well polished.

I bit. "Well, now," I said, my voice rising, "I have three Jewish daughters and I'm not sure I want them being led in Christian prayer every morning." By then, my wife was kicking me in the shin. My astonished teenage daughter watched the emerging drama, eyes anxiously wide.

"It would do them good," he spit. "Maybe they would learn about God."

I would have replied, but my wife's shoe on my shin was beginning to hurt. I would have told him that Jews invented God.

※

I don't know how we all fit into that little German car—my father, his wife, my wife, my youngest daughter, and me. We traveled across the Guadalajara Plateau toward Manzanillo on the *Golfo de California*. Banana plantations whizzed by as we descended from plateau to ocean. Unexpectedly—we had previously been

discussing landscapes—his wife said, "I think any man
who beats a woman should be strung up
by the thumbs." For the next several minutes I
experienced a new kind of silence. My wife, daughter
and I, sitting in the back seat, eyes quietly inflated,
stared at each other. Why did she say that? Did she not
know what had happened before her time? Was she
being intentionally provocative? What was *he* thinking?
Did he think I didn't remember? Did *he* remember?
Outside the car window, a speeding blur of green
banana leaves.

My father loved
Rush Limbaugh.

Using what he called the "Mexican National Flower,"
a satellite television reception disk, he'd never miss
Rush Limbaugh.

His face softened with a lovely, beatific smile for
Rush Limbaugh.

Recently, I felt that same warm-heart smile
flex my face. I was watching
pornography.

Baptizing Dad

I washed the old bastard's feet,
crusted, twisted and yellowed,
soaked them in warm soapy water
in a flowered Mexican bowl
from *la tienda* down the street.

What did I expect? That choirs
would open the skies, singing
my praise? That he would suddenly
become a decent man? That peace
would warm us in its fires?

Hey, Ram Dass, thanks,
but your suggestion—it didn't take.

It seemed like a good idea

Ridge running horses
sculpted from scrap
iron in the desert,
steely rusted steeds
racing sagebrush winds,
echoed memories
of when he was young.

"We could take him
out on the highway,
he could see it
one last time," maybe
die right there
by the roadside
watching running horses
going nowhere.

Last flower

Sitting in her wheel-chair, she held a yellow flower
in both hands. The first flower she had truly seen,
she was certain. Seventy-seven years old.

She adored that blossom, treasured its life.
By the time she died the following day,
she had forgotten the flower. Pain will do that.

She up and died

I'm sorry I got drunk
while you were dying.
Someone brought ice,
which made it seem
like a good idea.
That, and the Jack Daniels.
Or was it Jim Beam?
I don't remember, only know
I was in your room
but I wasn't with you.
Someone—my brother—
shook me awake. I rushed
to where you lay dead.

Death happens like that.
When you least expect it.

St. Joan

She fought the war, the tough war.
She won the war, terrible war.

A little country girl
leading the campaign
for truth, justice, honor,
for dignity and peace.

She died triumphant,
courageous, ready to go,
but charred to the bone.

My mother was Joan of Arc.

Swish of a horse's tail

Death is perfectly safe.

Stephen Levine, Year to Live:
How to Live This Year as if It Were Your Last

I intend to live forever, or die trying.

Groucho Marx

Cigarettes and wine

"I'm going for a walk," he said.
No you're not, she said.
You're going to the grocery store
to buy cigarettes and wine.
"You got me there," he said,
and off he went, flying away,
an athlete in night air,
stepping out with champion stride,
a speedy breeze to the minute mart.

Returning home, with a bottle
and a pack, he takes his time
past amber street lamps,
breathing in like a fat man
in a fat leather chair
in a rich private club
with a fat Cuban cigar,
shiny shoes on a shiny table
like nothing mattered.
The smoke filled his lungs
with cold stars and sky.

Davey's dance with the devil

Last night Davey tried re-enacting my father's death,
gurgling in bed, hacking, choking on phlegm
till his eyes fixed catatonic.

Davey rolled to the edge to expel
the pall of chronic pneumonia,
searched the air for air and wondered, *Is this it?*

This morning he held his canister close,
like a colostomy bag,
clear plastic tubes in his nostrils,
and told me *I'm so happy! I quit smoking!
Ten years ago today!*

Eddie Cotton, interrupted

You buy four burgers
but you get one more

at Eddie Cotton's burger store—the one on Madison—
where the welterweight contender tossed fat beef patties
and juicy hot links and bacon and cheese and lettuce
and tomatoes and bulging round brown buns for twenty
years after a steel beam fell fast as gravity on his fancy
left foot, forever knocking him out of the ring.

You buy five burgers
for the price of four.

The pianist

She sounded tubercular when she coughed
but he couldn't stay away.
She couldn't possibly be tubercular.
Besides, she was an easy lay.

He was autistic savant,
could not read her ways,
so she pulled him down, grabbed his cock
and pumped the night away.

At his next concert he coughed a bit
when he started to play.

With both feet on the floor,

sitting on the bed, his belly between his legs,
Bob wondered where everything went.
"It didn't used to be this way," he said aloud.
"I used to be able to find things easy.
I could show them off. Now, I haven't seen
my things in a couple of years. From what I can tell,
they aren't even the same things. It's like my things
left the planet before me. By the time I die,
I probably won't have a thing!"

Bob shrugged, looked out the window,
then to his cragged bare feet, brown toenails curled.
"On the other hand," he thought, "I don't need
so much anymore. Maybe a hug. A sunny day.
There comes a time when you don't
need things the way you used to."

He put the revolver back in the drawer.

The murderer upstairs

> *Police found my friend Michael burning in the back seat of a yellow Mercury Capri, hands tied behind his back, bullet hole in his head.*

The murderer upstairs
lives on the seventh floor.
When he pulls one off,
he showers with hot foggy water
while my window gathers icy rain.
Cold rills chase gravity on glass.
In my bare room, I hear his pounding
spray, scorching his shower floor.
The wet winds of *Njord* assault my window.

Tucson

> *January 8, 2011. Attempted assassination of Democratic Congresswoman Gabrielle Giffords. The murder of a dozen, including a Federal judge and a nine-year-old girl.*

The dead people don't say anything.
They just lie around the shopping mall,
wishing they wore clean underwear that day.
The gun with the hot barrel didn't know
what happened. It just felt good,
shooting off that way.
Gun sales shot higher than the Arizona sun.

Boom boom boom.
Can't get enough
can't get enough
of that bang bang stuff.

Boom boom boom.
Gotta get more
gotta get down
to the bang bang store.

Boom boom boom.
Gotta get a bang bang
gotta get a gun
gotta be a hero
have some fun.

Boom boom boom.
Holster on my hip
looks real neat
gotta get a gun
pack some heat
a little bit of bang-a-bang
can't be beat.

Boom boom boom.
Gotta get guns
gotta get a lot
gonna make bang-a-bang
in a parking lot.

Boom boom boom.
Gotta hear the bang-a-bang
Gotta hear it loud
Gotta make a bang-a-bang
in a big crowd.

Boom boom boom
Boom boom boom.

Can't get enough
of that bang-a-bang stuff.

Boom boom boom.
Boom boom boom.
Boom.   Boom.   Boom.
                            Boom.

A terrible mistake

The last of the Culbertson family

Corroded chrome on an old Oldsmobile
fender rusting in the horse pasture
behind my grandfather's cabin,
hidden in tall grass waving in summer;

the horses, sold long ago.

Blood on my shirt sleeve, still wet,
Merlot splashes on the ragged wood floor,
yellowed kitchen sink turned red as cherries,
fresh from the orchard behind the barn.

Endings are always difficult.

It wasn't meant to be this way.
Photographs weren't meant to fade
or burn the way the cabin burns tonight.
Lovers don't leave, children don't die.

Life should be pretty.

When first they met

He dies in his dreams.
She embalms his body
on the stainless slab,
touching him softly,
like putting a baby
to sleep on the beach,
again and again.

He dies in her dreams.
She washes his body
stretched out in the lab,
soaping him softly,
a repeated spiritual rite
that she too dreams
again and again.

The end of summer

But the time is past for living in a dream world.
Leon Russell, *Will o' the Wisp*, "Back to the Island"

Not far from the Pacific Crest Trail,
the one that wanders along ridges
from Canadian Cascades south
to the Californian Sierras, past rocks
grey in the north, beige in the south,
in a dark fir refuge we met the body
of a man, brains blown away, lying
in the forest duff (a chipmunk near),
fresh laundered jeans and blood,
a nasty blue jay razzing above.
We found a tree-nailed note,
on sweat stained paper:

It was wonderful. All of it.
Wouldn't have missed any of it.
You, every one of you, were special.
You delighted me and I love you.
Life is beautiful. Unforgettable.
I apologize for my abrupt exit.
I just had to go back to my island.

Wisdom of the wind

Watching leaves waving in the wind,
what a wonderful thing. I watch them often,
remembering my neighbor who found leaves
on the hood of his Buick, departing his driveway
one autumn morning. As he picked up speed,
he noticed the leaves fluttering.
Driving faster, golden leaves flew from the hood.
Inspired by the thought of removing all the leaves
with mere wind power, he pulled onto the freeway.
A few leaves stayed stuck, so he floor-boarded
the gas and at 100 miles per hour
he rear-ended a truck loaded with explosives.
He died, of course,
watching leaves waving in the wind.

When Buddha Dog died,

I drank until two in the morning
first with Mona, then Nick,
the way I drank when my parents
died, both mysteries to me,
endearments hidden, dreams unspoken,
protected by bristling barriers,
unlike The Buddha Dog,
who showed me his heart
until his last breath.

Dog gone

1.
Black furry balls in the corners
remain three days later,
dog dish in the kitchen,
leash on the counter.
Still.

2.
Rising from sofa or bed,
take care, don't step
on the animal
that isn't there.
Get the morning paper
yourself.

3.
Knock on the door, ring the bell.
I don't care. The dog won't bark.
He isn't there.

4.
Sit on the deck in the sunshine
alone.
Move from to room to room
alone.
Walk around the block
alone.
No animal begs to come
along.

5.
No nose nudges my elbow
at five o'clock feeding time.

6.
He's gone.

Lamplight lamentation

For Cousin Jimmy

He sat at a narrow table, a kerosene lamp at his side.
He placed a thin writing pad on the rough surface,
removed a fountain pen from his pocket
and wrote:

> I often see young women.
> They give me massages and pedicures.
> Women's hands touch me that way.
> Waitresses greet me at the café
> where you and I ate eggs-over-easy.
> They are kind, the way they touch me
> on the shoulder and sometimes wink.
> At the market they remember me, my name,
> ask me about my day, warming me
> with their lipstick smiles.
> Young women are so vital!
> But they will not, cannot, replace you.
> I will miss you forever.

His hands were cold and cramped. It was late.
He turned to the cot beside the table and slept.

What a lovely way

He sang,
"Uh-huh,
she don't
like it
like that."

He shook a tambourine, slapped it on his thigh. The band played and he flashed his best bumping smile with some ready in his eye. The crowd clapped and chanted, "Uh-huh, she don't like it like that!" Glittering women cooed background harmony. The stage became panty-land. They tossed 'em up for the sweating, gravelly voiced man—urging him to lift them higher. The club pulsed, "Uh-huh, she don't like it like that!" Over and over. Yes, over and over. Heavy bass and drums. Always drums. The song grew long. It went on. And on. The crowd roared. Sweat poured. Till he became a pile on the floor. Not breathing.

Uh-huh,
she don't
like it
like that.

These times

Channeling Utah Phillips

Burning buildings in foreign lands!
Tyrants bought the money men,
not cheap dealers in alleys
but big boss bankers, phallic corporations.

Third world in heat, fucking world-wide,
lubricated by oil, shooting big guns.
They want to come, come big in your life.
Big buck moguls, commanders of cash,

don't give a rat's rectum about you,
your children, parents, anyone dear.
You are a *human resource*
to exploit, not a corporate person.

My children, remember your grandfather,
remember the words on the makeshift sign
held in his bloodied hands when he died:
Don't trust the damn corporations.

Another one

With a soft surging sound
Eldon hit the ground
twenty years old—
     raised on television
     and weight rooms
an all-American kid, his mother said
natural born leader, his friend Ben said
a damn good soldier, his sergeant said.

With a soft surging sound
Eldon entered the ground
a beautiful cemetery—
     with white markers
     and green knolls
not far from where we live, his father said
a view of the river, his sweetheart said
his own marble marker, the Reverend said.

Remembering Frank

Frank died a week or two ago,
maybe three, more or less,
not that it surprised anyone
who had seen him struggling,
his weakened weightless body
dropping to the ground
to trim garden hedges
on his hands and knees,
scolding his nieces
for not pruning correctly.

Neighbor Phil stopped by
today to remind me I failed
to attend Frank's funeral
and to see if I knew what
will happen to Frank's house.
"People are saying he was
hard to get along with," Phil said.
He was a fussbudget, I replied,
That's not the same. "Yeah,"
said Phil, "He was a fussbudget."
There's a difference, I said.

Remembering George

My friend George,
he's dead. Suicide.

I remember walking
with him on a sunny day,
music surrounding us,
a folk festival of peace.

I told him I thought
I would like to go national,
create a product or an idea
that would propel me toward
comfort the way Gildna Radner
bought a New England estate
by starring in a supporting role
for an ordinary-but-national film.

He replied: *I want to know
what it feels like to be a woman.*
Really, I said, you want to change?
*Only for a day. I want to be a woman
for a day, to feel it in my skin.*
This annoyed me, how he ignored
the fact my fantasy could happen
and his could not.

Suicide. Imagine that.

Better late than never

Aging comes sooner than expected,
sweeps in like a high plains blizzard,
turns the sky, air, everything, white—
confounding all sense of direction,
like late-night stumbling home
from a wonderful party,
lost and dependent on others,
trying to remember a lifetime,
before the storm hit.

Say goodbye now

The incandescence of life
burns out like pyres in night.
Like that, you're gone.
It will happen in spite

of your desire or faith
or your mistakes atoned.
It will happen, you're gone.
Like that, you're home.

NOTES

1.
The last two lines of "The evening of the day after things changed like they'd never changed before" *echo the first chorus in Jerry Jeff Walker's* "I feel like Hank Williams Tonight," Tried and True Music, 1989:

>And I play classical music when it rains,
>I play country when I am in pain.
>But I won't play Beethoven, the mood's just not right
>Oh, I feel like Hank Williams tonight.

2.
Regarding "Another One": *The first line of this poem is inspired by the last verse of Charles Simic's* "October Arriving" (The Voice at 3:00 AM: Selected Late and New Poems (Harcourt, Inc., 2003).

>Dark masses of trees
>Cast their mazes before him,
>Only to erase them next
>With a sly, sea-surging sound.

3.
Regarding "The First Noble Truth": *There is suffering. First, there is the pain or suffering of birth, disease, injury, aging, illness, distress, dying and so on, often called* "ordinary suffering." *Translators choose the word* "suffering" *to represent the Sanskrit and Pali words* dukkha *and* duhka, *which convey more than mere physical suffering. Dukkha includes mental suffering—loneliness, disappointment, fear, anger, hatred, as well as dread and doubt. Buddhism teaches that our suffering is based on our desire for things to be otherwise and on our failure to comprehend the universality of impermanence.*

4.
Mark Sandman, fronting his band Morphine, died July 3, 1999 from a heart attack on stage at the Giardini del Principe *in Palestrina, Italy. He*

was 46. The poem "What a lovely way" does not reflect his style of music but certainly expresses my shock when he died.

5.
The album cover for B.B. King and Eric Clapton's Grammy-winning collaboration, "Riding with the King" (Reprise, 2000), depicted the two musicians relaxing and laughing in a luxury convertible; Clapton driving, King sprawled in back. It inspired the poem "Eric Clapton, B.B. King, and me." B.B. King died the day I wrote this sentence.

6.
"Eddie Cotton, interrupted" and "What a lovely way" each experiment with the interrupted monosonnet form sometimes used by Sherman Alexie.

7.
The poems "Broken" and "My parents' house" recall my mother's attempted suicide. I was seventeen. My six-year-old brother found her.

8.
The third section title in this collection comes from a Buddhist saying used by Jack Kornfield: "Winds of karma change like the swish of a horse's tail."

9.
While preparing this book, seven friends who died too soon were on my mind: Richard, Kerry Ann, Jane, George, Kimo, Michael and Craig. Three by cancer, two by suicide, one by murder, one by clearing brush.

10.
All my gratitude to Celia, Wally, Mrs. Bloomquist, Bernice, Pamela, Shar, Mike, Scott, and Kate—especially Kate—for your encouragement and support.

ABOUT THE AUTHOR

Originally from the Oregon side of Hells Canyon, North America's deepest gorge, Tito Titus lives with his wife Kate near Puget Sound in Washington state. A retired quasi-judicial environmental hearings examiner, he also worked as a farmhand, range-fire fighter, carnival barker, soldier, art model, environmental activist, urban planner, and Seattle Design Commissioner.

His poems appear in *The Little Red Anthology,* Paco-Michelle Atwood's *World Inside Designer Jeans,* and *Red Light District: Seattle Erotic Art Festival 2011 Literary Anthology*. From 2004 to 2012, he regularly performed his poetry at Seattle's Little Red Studio and with Floating Mountain Poets.

His social and political satire appeared in *Seattle Post-Intelligencer, Puget Soundings* and *Argus*. Washington State's King County honored him with its Martin Luther King, Jr. Humanitarian Award for his service to elderly homeless people.